The Shining Hour of Departure

By Hannah Hurnard

"Through cloud and sunshine,
oh, abide with me!"

The Shining Hour of Departure
by Hannah Hurnard Introduction by Jeanne Saul

ISBN-13: 978-1511895002
ISBN-10: 1511895004

First printing 2012 Second Printing 2015
Printed in the United States of America

Firestarter Publications P. O. Box 961 Huntsville, Arkansas 72740, Firestarterpublications.com

This little book is a published letter written by Hannah Hurnard. Firestarter Publications has put it into a paperback form so that it can be easily given away.

Introduction

Hannah Hurnard has best been remembered by her classic book *Hinds Feet in High Places* . The story is about a girl named "Much-Afraid" who lives in the "Valley of Humiliation"., she loves the Shepherd with all of her heart and desires to be in His service. She longs to have "hind's feet" and "leap upon the high places" with Him. It has the flavor of Pilgrims Progress but easier to follow. Hannah Hurnard (1905-1990) was born in Colchester, England to Quaker parents. Graduated from Ridgelands Bible College of Great Britain in 1926. In 1932 she became an independent missionary for 50 years in Haifa, Israel. She maintained a home in England as well

Unlike many of Hurnards books that followed *Hinds Feet in High Places* , The Shining Hour of Departure simply gives us the facts about aging and coming to grips with our usefulness in the Kingdom of God up to the very end. It does not go into any of the theological stances that had become so controversial. This special letter written in her later years says this: "For several years I had been conscious that more and more of my rather older friends, and even some younger ones, had been taking their departure from this World, and, not infrequently, amongst those who remained, I had heard such wistful remarks as these, "Well, of course one can't expect to do as much now as when one was younger," or "One doesn't want to have to lay everything down, you know, and to have nothing left. It's difficult to find oneself laid aside and 'put on the shelf.' It's lonely when the friends of your own generation have all gone and the children are grown up and living lives of their own.". But then she goes on to say: "Being an example and inspiration and strengthener of the weak, simply by being a demonstration of the grace and love of the Lord who calls us to follow the way that He went."

I came across this letter written by Hannah Hurnard on a website. It was titled *The Shinning Hour of Departure*. I fell in love with it right away as I was caring for many elderly and hospice patients at that time. I printed it out and read it to many of my patients. They were so encouraged and enlightened. I gave away many copies. I realized how it spoke in such a strong way to the fear of being "useless" or the fear of being told "You only have so long to live", that it had to be made available in paperback. Now it can be given to those who need encouragement at this beautiful time in their lives.

Jeanne Saul

The Shining Hour of Departure

"Do you see yonder shining light?"
(Bunyan's Pilgrim's Progress.)

A few weeks ago I received a courteous letter from The Ministry of Pensions. It informed me that it will no longer be necessary for me to send in an application for my Old Age Pension each quarter, as I have done for the past five years, nor will a statement concerning possible extra earnings, be needed. All that will be required of me in the future will be a confirmation, from time to time, that I am still alive and eligible for the Pension.

The receipt of this letter (which, strangely enough) I had not been expecting, had a most exhilarating effect upon me. It was as though I had suddenly reached a Sign Post, announcing that I am beginning a completely new phase in the great adventure of this "Journey of Life" here on earth. I have really reached the frontiers of "Old Age" and, somewhere beyond them, lie those other frontiers— those of my real "Home Country" from which I have been absent for sixty-five earth years. Certainly I must begin to consider the meaning and purpose of this new and exciting phase of the last part of the journey, before the hour comes when I must depart out of this World and go to our Father. John 13:1.

As this dawned upon me, my heart tingled with a mixture of longing and excitement. Now it must surely be right and permissible to let myself think of the joy and rapture of the arrival back at my true Home! To let my "heart wax warm at the thought of where I am going" as

Bunyan's Pilgrim described it. To the Land from which I came I am returning, and surely all sorts of joyful, though secret, preparations should be made. To tell the truth, ever since childhood, for some reason or other, I have never really felt at home here on Earth. Almost as though I were a child who, having failed the end of term examination at school, instead of passing on to a fuller and richer life in a higher World, had been obliged to return to Earth for another term at school to see if I could do better.

Yes, the letter from the Ministry of Pensions "pulled me up short," in a very unexpected and delightful manner. It made me say to myself, "Ah, my soul! you will soon be standing at the door of our Father's House," not only running joyfully in to be welcomed, but also to hand in the "School Report." So I had better begin checking up to see if there are any important lessons I have short-changed, or have not properly mastered; to consider how the last part of this adventurous and tremendous journey can be the sweetest, richest, happiest and most fruitful of all. Yes, I had better begin consulting my older friends and making inquiries about the best way to grow old beautifully and happily; to discover if there is such a thing as a real "Ministry of Old Age" and, if so, how to enter upon it.

For several years I had been conscious that more and more of my rather older friends, and even some younger ones, had been taking their departure from this World, and, not infrequently, amongst those who remained, I had heard such wistful remarks as these, "Well, of course one can't expect to do as much now as when one was younger," or "One doesn't want to have to lay everything down, you know, and to have nothing left.

It's difficult to find oneself laid aside and 'put on the shelf.' It's lonely when the friends of your own generation have all gone and the children are grown up and living lives of their own." Gradually, one special question had been forming in my mind, as I watched others passing through the experience of Old Age, "If sight and hearing have almost gone, and weakness and physical infirmities increase and there is nothing left but TIME, what does one do with one's TIME? How should one spend it?"

Obviously it was now high time to begin making inquiries, and the first person I approached was a sweet faced old lady approaching her ninetieth birthday. She lives in a Home for retired people, and, to tell the truth, I had heard that some of the other elderly people who lived there were not very happy about the way it was run. So while we were having lunch together, I began my questioning. How did she like living where she now was, instead of in her own home?

Her face lighted up as she said happily, "Oh, I can't speak too highly of this place. Everybody is so kind, and we are so well cared for." I was a little disconcerted at hearing this different version of the case, and said tentatively, "I have heard that there is a continual change of staff. Different wardens and helpers coming and going all the time?"

"Well, that is so," she conceded cheerily. "It seems very difficult nowadays to find any permanent helpers. But while they are with us they are all very nice and kind. For instance, the nurse who is with us at present is very young indeed. She looks a mere girl, and one would think she would find it very dull and dreary looking after old people. But you know she is just lovely to me. It seems that there is nothing that is too much trouble for her to do."

I looked at the sweet, contented, old face before me and made a mental note. It seems that if you learn to be contented, grateful and appreciative you help to bring the best out in other people, and you are not likely to have a lonely and neglected old age. Especially if you also learn to ignore quietly, and without protest, the things you find not very much to your liking, and <u>concentrate on making the best of everything.</u>

As I had obviously found an expert authority on the subject, I said, "Please will you give me your advice as to the best preparations I can make for enjoying a peaceful, happy and fruitful old age." Like most old people, her thoughts moved more slowly than before. She was silent for a few moments and a faraway look came into her eyes, as though she were looking back through the years at the long journey behind her. Then she said:

"I don't think one can make any special preparations. Things happen, you know, that you can't foresee. But remember, there is something new every day, if you look for it." Ah, yes! Every day God sends us new tokens of His loving kindness and tender mercy. How wonderful to be able to reassure ourselves that, right through to the end of life here on earth each day will bring us new blessings and joys if we are on the watch for them. Looking for Him to come with just the new grace and support we need. Something brought to us, perhaps by some invisible angel or heavenly messenger, to gladden each day and prevent the feeling of loneliness when bereaved of lost friends and departed joys. To be on the watch each day for new happy things, and to disregard the things we would not have chosen, and so rejoicing in the sunshine of His love, to let "the fruits of the Spirit-love, joy, peace, long-suffering, gentleness, goodness, faith, meekness and self-control" ripen in us to full maturity and mellowness. Gal. 5:22,23.

I thanked my friend and stored her secret in my heart. Then I went to visit a very special friend of mine, with whom I have lived and worked for the four happiest years of my life in the Holy Land. She is eighty-six now, and for a good many years past has been living in a flat of her own, with kind neighbors and friends close at hand. As she opened the door to me, a strong smell of burning swept out into the hall. "Oh, Hannah, darling," she said, regretfully and yet quite cheerily, "I have reached the stage when I forget everything. I put the potatoes in the casserole in the oven, and they are all scorched to cinders on one side. But we can cut the bottoms off and eat the tops! How lovely it is to see you!"

She could not hear a word I said until she had found and adjusted her "hearing aid," and her dear, kind eyes could not easily see the love with which I was regarding her. But as we ate together the meal which her love had provided, I eagerly asked my questions. We were such old friends that I felt quite free to tell her all that was in my heart, and even to speak of what the radio recently called, "The Unmentionable Subject" of one's own passing from this world to the next. "Peace," I said (that is not her name but it well describes her), "Do you still read Bunyan's Pilgrim's Progress, especially the part about the pilgrims coming to Beulah Land, on the edge of the River, before they crossed over to the Celestial City? We read that in Beulah Land they anointed themselves ready for their departure from this world, and there they felt as if they were in heaven even before they reached it."

"Oh, yes," said Peace, instantly. I turn to that again and again, even though I can do very little reading now. The River can't come too soon for me, Hannah, but I am very happy while I wait to cross over." "What makes you so happy?" I asked. She did not hesitate for a moment. "As long as you have someone to love, and to be loved by," she said, "you cannot help being happy."

For a moment I was almost taken aback. For Peace, like myself, is unmarried. She has no lifelong companion, and no children to comfort her old age. All the friends of her own generation have passed on into the World of Light. She herself was the youngest member of a family of twelve and is the only one left. Then who was there left for her to love and to be loved by?

Well, the answer soon became quite clear. Everyone she met and heard about seemed to come into one or other of the necessary categories! Moreover, she had one special niece who had been living near her, but now was preparing to move to the other side of the country and wanted to make a home for her there. "I don't know any body in those parts," said Peace, "but my friends think I am getting too old and forgetful to live alone any longer and it will be lovely to live with her. I shall have to let go all these things in the flat," she went on cheerfully, "even my precious books. But there! I can hardly see to read them, and all my real treasures are waiting for me in heaven. So, when it is time to be off I shall go with great joy. Of course, Hannah, I do sometimes feel a little lonely and terribly useless, but if you love you can't stay lonely and unhappy. Remembering others and thinking about them lovingly, is something I can still do."

Has Old Age a special Ministry? Yes, I realized joyfully, it certainly has. It is no longer the Ministry of DOING, but the Ministry of BEING—

Being a beautiful example of what the grace and love of God can do in a human life, right through to the end of it, changing it little by little into "a burning bush" of love— BEING someone who inspires in others a wonderful sense of confidence in God's unchanging love, goodness and faithfulness— Being a continual reassurance to others, not so far on in the journey, that He who has called us to follow our Lord and Master and to grow like Him, is able to do it; to demonstrate right through to the end that God's faithfulness never fails and He never disappoints our hopes.

I remember, long ago in 1924, when, as a morbid, miserable girl of nineteen, handicapped by a humiliating stammer, and just struggling out of a nervous breakdown, I went with my father to the Keswick Convention. And there the transforming miracle happened. The love of God, "in the face of Jesus Christ," shone into my lonely, frightened heart, and Charles Wesley's hymn became real in my own experience:

> "Long my imprisoned spirit lay
> Fast bound in chains of deepest night;
> Thine eye diffused a quickening ray,
> I woke, the dungeon flamed with light.
> My chains fell off, my soul went free,
> I rose, went forth and followed Thee."

My feet actually stood at last, on the shining path along which my Lord and Saviour has been leading me since, (for forty-five years) a path truly growing brighter with every year that passes.

But did anyone, I wonder, ever start more trembling **to** follow Him than I did? I remember looking out on eager, happy faces of the hundreds of other young people who attended the special evening meetings for Youth, many of whom had testified to yielding their lives to God during the Convention. I thought fearfully to myself, "I wonder how long they will keep following? How many of them will presently turn back? Will this wonderful new joy in my own heart really last? Will the Lord be able to keep me delivered from the dungeons of Fearing Castle and from those old, dreadful depressions, for even one week? Or will it all vanish away like a dream?

Then, as I sat in the tent, I looked at the faces of some of the "really old" Convention speakers on the platform, with their white hair and aging bodies. I noted the joy and peace in their faces, and listened to the glad confidence with which they spoke, and I remember how my heart leaped hopefully within me as I thought to myself, "Well the Lord has certainly kept them for a great many years. He has not failed them during their long journey through this frightening world. They are still radiant and victorious even in old age. Surely He will not want to fail me either." I remember how comforted I felt as I turned from the eager young faces, to the reassuringly happy and strong faces of those older men, and I think that was the first moment when I realized that even old age has a special and beautiful ministry of its own, one which no other age can fulfill so triumphantly;

the ministry of being an inspiration and reassurance to the inexperienced younger folk as they start on the untried way. Seen in this light, Old Age is one of the most responsible and blessed periods in life— being an example and inspiration and strengthener of the weak, simply by being a demonstration of the grace and love of the Lord who calls us to follow the way that He went.

Shortly after my visit to Peace, I was walking one day in the fields near my childhood's home, and found myself approaching a glorious old tree which must have been growing there for at least two hundred years. It was a mellow, sunny afternoon at the end of the summer, and the great, spreading branches of the tree were still covered with rich foliage, and the birds were coming and going around it. As I drew near, I found myself speaking to the tree and saying, "Please will you tell me your prescription for growing old as beautifully as you have done."

The tree answered me at once and said quite clearly, "If you are willing to give loving shelter and welcome to all the creatures that come to you; excluding none and differentiating between none; if you keep open to the light continually; and, if you are willing to let everything go at the right time, you cannot fail to have a happy and blessed Old Age like mine." I thanked the old tree from the bottom of my heart and thought over those three vital points.

1. Willingness to give a loving welcome to all who come seeking for the shelter of an understanding heart. I remembered what Peace had said, "If you have someone to love and to be loved by, you can never be really lonely and unhappy." And I prayed, "Dear Lord, please teach

me to welcome everyone and to think lovingly about them. Help me to forgive those who hurt me, or seem to neglect me; forgive them, not just for the things they say and do, but, also, for being the sort of people they are, and cannot help being."

2. Always keep open to new light from God. I thought of the words of my other old friend who had said, "Remember there is something new every day. Be on the watch for it." I prayed, "Dear Lord, please help me to keep looking for all the happy, good things that happen, and to rejoice in them most gratefully and thankfully, and help me to ignore and refuse to think about the things I don't like and which seem difficult and dreary."

3. Be willing to let everything go at the right time, as the trees so beautifully let go of all their leafy treasures, allowing them to drop off, and sealing over the vacant spot so that not a pang of loss remains. Let them go as sweetly as Peace was preparing to do, as she was about to be uprooted from her beloved little home and to be transplanted to a strange new environment where there would be no room for her old treasures. To loosen one's roots from earthly things, in order to put them down more and more strongly in the higher heavenly world hidden beyond the veil of our physical sight. Beginning to make that world more real to our inner consciousness than this earthly one is to our bodily senses.

But how can one do that? Nowadays there seems to be a conspiracy of silence on this subject, as though the very idea of thinking happily about our real Homeland or "the World to come," while we are still in this one, is in some way unseemly and morbid. We are told that in olden times (I don't know if the practice is still continued) the monks in very strict Carmelite Orders, slept each night in their coffins, and kept a skull in each cell, so that they could, in this way, familiarize themselves with the thought of death and with the fleeting temporality of this life.

It is easy to call such a custom a morbid and unhealthy preoccupation with death. But I really wonder if it is any more morbid and unhealthy than refusing altogether to think about the future hour of our departure from this world, or to talk to one another about dying, utterly refusing to familiarize ourselves with the wonderful and inescapable event with which each one of us will be confronted sometime— our departure from this world into the next: The putting off of these mortal, physical bodies, in order to put on our new, immortal, heavenly bodies, so that we may enter rejoicing into an incomparably richer form of life in a higher, heavenly world.

Surely it is a strangely morbid and unhealthy thing to be afraid to mention death to the dying; to make it the "unmentionable subject" which it has become. The early Christians, constantly persecuted and confronted as they continually were with the threat of death, adopted quite a different attitude towards it. Instead of seeking to escape from all thoughts about it, they confronted it bravely and looked it full in the face, and saw it for what it really is, an old Scarecrow— a defeated foe, a "nothing" dressed up as though it were something terrible. For them, the death and resurrection of Jesus had unveiled the glorious truth; that death has been swallowed up in victory. It's not what men have fearfully thought it to be. It is simply the physical process of putting off an outworn mortal garment in order to put on a new immortal one in which to "Passover" (lovely name for what we call death) into the real world, compared to which this world is only like a dream one.

So the early Christians familiarized themselves with the idea. They talked about it together and sang about it most joyfully, and made hopeful preparations, so that, however suddenly and unexpectedly it might come, they would be all ready to take their departure, with everything left well arranged and as easy as possible to deal with by those who were left behind. Their loved ones were constantly being carried off to prison, and then violently deprived of their physical bodies, and no one knew when his own turn would come. That is why they learned to confront the idea joyfully and hopefully and to prepare for it gladly. That was why they so exulted in the resurrection of Jesus, for it was glorious proof that death really is only a door into the Higher World, rather like another birth out of the womb of this earth into the World of Heaven. So the idea of "Passing Over" became as familiar and joyful an idea to them as is the prospect of returning home for the holidays to the child at boarding school. How strange and sad that, in our day and generation, this attitude seems to be so altered.

Like Bunyan's Pilgrim, I myself want to let "my thought wax warm about where I am going," and, like countless pilgrims before me, make secret, happy plans for the glorious coming change and my arrival back in my real Homeland.

One morning, a few days after talking to the beautiful old tree and to the two beautiful old friends, whom I have mentioned, I woke from sleep with a verse from John's Gospel shining into my mind. "Before the Feast of the Passover, when Jesus KNEW THAT HIS HOUR WAS COME, THAT HE SHOULD DEPART OUT OF THIS WORLD to the Father, having loved His own which were in the world, HE LOVED THEM UNTO THE END." John 13:1. "The hour had come," (as it will come, some day, to each one of us) that He should depart out of this world. How did He prepare for it? Why just at this particular point, does it say these beautiful words? "Having loved His own which were in the world, He loved them unto the end."

As I thought about the words, it came to me most vividly that He well knew that His departure from this world would be through the door of an agonizing death, hanging for hours on a cross, experiencing the most terrible form of death that fallen human beings have ever invented. But HE did not spend a single moment thinking about it, nor picturing what it would be like, nor living over and over again in anticipation, the horrors to come. No indeed; all His thoughts were centered on one thing thinking lovingly and com-passionately about His friends and their needs and picturing the best way to help those who, not realizing it, were so soon to be bereaved of the heavenly joy and assurance and security of His physical presence. No terrible imaginations were allowed to form in His mind; all His mental powers were employed in loving others and thinking about them. This continued right through "to the end" —even when He was hanging on the cross. So strong and serene, and even joyful in this redemptive Ministry of Love, He could go forth unafraid to meet what was coming, assured that when "the hour came," He would be succored and brought through everything in triumph.

These thoughts bring me naturally to consider the chief natural reasons why death has become an "unmentionable subject," so fearful an idea that human beings do not like to speak about it to each other. So many of us are terrified at the thought of the suffering that may precede it; the long, lingering illness, cancer, a stroke, paralysis, complete helplessness, blindness, deafness, failing strength, unbearable pain. That is what causes death to seem so terrible to many people. The Bible is very tender and understanding on this subject. It speaks compassionately of those "who through fear of death were all their lifetime subject to bondage" Heb. 2:15 and promises that we can be delivered from that fear by the Lord "Who, through death, destroyed its power." I, myself, for a long time, was very much afraid of dying. Like many others who possess a vivid imagination, I was tempted to picture to myself the whole process of lingering disease and death, and to shrink in terror from it. I was the kind of person who even dreaded the thought of going to sit down in the dentist's chair if there was something a little unpleasant or painful for him to do.

I well remember the occasion years ago, when a middle-aged woman came to me after I had been speaking at a meeting, and said to me in a trembling voice, as she caught hold of my hands, "Hannah, I have cancer, and the doctors say that they cannot operate. I am simply terrified. There is such a little time left. Can no one do anything to help me and to keep me alive?"

A pang went right through my own heart. I could picture and feel exactly how she felt: just how I would be feeling myself if I were in her place. I could only put my arms around her and say, with tears of compassion, "Oh, I really am certain that when you reach the time you so much dread, you will find the loving Lord and Saviour there, waiting to help you and to carry you right through in triumph, and without fear. He will not fail you if you cast yourself upon Him and seek His help. Once I too had to have an operation (though not for cancer) and I was dreadfully afraid until I reached the operating theatre, and then— there He was, and all the fear went, swallowed up in peace. I am sure it will be the same for you, because you see, He loves us and delights in helping us if we will give Him the opportunity to do so.

Then I told her about an old friend of my mother's, who, many years ago, was dying with cancer. She sent a message asking me to go and see her. I was only a very young Christian and was dreadfully afraid seeing pain, and I shrank from going. But when I entered her room I saw her lying on the bed (almost at the end of the journey) and her face was simply radiant. She did not speak to me about herself at all, but only asked for news about myself and the other members of the family. I was only allowed to stay for a few minutes, and then the nurse beckoned me from the room. But there was one question I simply had to ask before I left— never to see her again. So I said, "They tell me that you are nearly always in great pain (this was nearly forty years ago). Please, please will you tell me how you bear it? For I am so dreadfully afraid of pain myself."

Her face lit up. "So was I," she said. "I have always been afraid of dying because of the pain that might precede it. I feared that the pain would be so great that it would make it impossible for me to realize the Presence of my Lord, and that I should be crazed by it. I was afraid that even He would not be able to keep me in peace and joy and contact with Himself in the fires of suffering. But, Hanna, it has all been so different to what I feared and imagined; for never in all my life before has His Presence been so real to me and His peace and joy so great, as now. I am truly glad that He let me come this way, because I could never have known how wonderful He is, and how absolutely sufficient His grace can be."

Then she asked me to pick up the Bible which was lying open on the table beside her, and to read the verse which was underlined on that page. I did so and read these words, "Beloved, think it not strange concerning the fiery trial which is to try you, as though some strange thing happened unto you; but rejoice, inasmuch as ye are partakers of Christ's sufferings; that when His glory shall be revealed ye shall be glad also with exceeding joy." 1 Peter 4:12, 13.

"Those words have returned to me again and again. They formed, indeed, the first step on the pathway of escape from my own fear of death and of pain. They helped me to believe, that no matter how I may feel beforehand, when I get to the situation I have so much dreaded and may have been tempted to picture with fear and dismay, I shall find that He really is there, all ready to bear me safely through. He has never been known to fail the weak and the fearful who seek His aid. How I love the words which John Bunyan put into the mouth of Mr. Great-Heart when he was describing the journey of Mr. Fearing to the Celestial City. Mr. Fearing, he tells us, was all through his journey, terrified by everything he pictured and supposed would happen to him, especially as he drew near to the River which had to be crossed before the City could be reached. He was certain that he would be lost forever in the River and never reach the goal of his heart's desire. "But our Lord is of very tender compassions towards them that are afraid," said Mr. Great-Heart, "and I took note that when Mr. Fearing entered the river, it was at lower ebb than I ever saw it before or since, so he crossed over, almost dry shod."

Isn't that lovely! Indeed our Lord IS of very tender compassions to them that fear. I know this from my own experience —again and again. I have found it true that He does not despise us for our fears. He does not add to them by chidingly warning us that we bring upon ourselves the very things we fear. Absolutely not; He knows that we cannot help our fears, and without Him we cannot "pull ourselves together" and escape from their clutches. He understands perfectly, and He succors us, and from my own oft repeated experiences of His grace and help, I can testify that "Better hath He been for years, than my fears!" Again and again I have exclaimed with thankful, exulting joy, "This is the 'tomorrow' that I so much dreaded— and it hasn't happened! Praise Him!"

Before passing from this subject of pain and suffer there is one gloriously comforting and wonderful point which I would like to emphasize. If it should be that our path does lie through the Valley of Suffering, or through some fiery furnace, or the wilderness of loneliness or sorrow, we may remind our self of a glorious truth. **NO, SUFFERING IS USELESS**. If God did not use it in wondrous ways, He would not permit it to exist. If it was useless, it would never be allowed to come our way. But all suffering is a mighty energy and power which God uses in redemptive ways to bless us and countless others know nothing about. It was certainly not God's first will that suffering should exist or manifest in any form. But since the Fall, when Mankind departed from God's will and purpose, suffering has been the mighty energy which God redeems us and draws poor Mankind back to Himself. The cross is the revelation that the Divine Loving consciousness of God suffers with us and in us. "In all our afflictions He is afflicted" and the angel of His Presence (His own consciousness projected into us) delivers us. Not only that, He uses the energy of Suffering to help save others. Only this morning, as I listened to the "Ten to Eight" radio talk I heard words which beautifully sum up what I am trying to say. "God shares the sufferings of His creatures...If we offer our sufferings to Christ, He USES them in the work of redeeming the world." How glorious this thought should sustain and comfort us. He can use our sufferings, our loneliness, our sorrow, and all our tribulations, just as wonderfully as He graciously chooses to use the glad active service we may have been privileged to offer Him at other times.

I think another thing about Death and "the hour of departure from this world" that we are tempted to dread, is the fact that we feel we do not know anything about what lies beyond Death. When we put off these mortal bodies, it means that we pass beyond the reach of everything familiar, out into a completely unknown world and surroundings— and the unknown terrifies some of us very much indeed. But I wonder if this too is really only another old bogey! For remember, really we are only returning to where we came from. Our spirits have all come from God, "The Father of spirits" Hebrews 12:9 and we are going back to Him and to Our "Father's House" to hand in our school reports and to receive His loving welcome.

I myself have a joyful suspicion that the nearer we get to the frontiers of that other world, the more familiar it will become. It is only when we are far away from the Home Land and absorbed in earthly things, that the heavenly realities seem unfamiliar to us. I remember how my heart used to thrill while I was sitting in the train returning from school to my hometown for the holidays. At first all the country I passed through was unfamiliar because it was so distant from Colchester. But as we drew nearer I began to see the first familiar landmarks which made me recognize that I was getting very near home. How eagerly I would look out of the train window, and then suddenly exclaim to myself with ecstatic joy, "Oh look! There is dear old Jumbo-the water tower, and the spire of the Town Hall— and now we are passing over 'The Seven Arches'— and there is the river flowing through the meadows, and there is dear 'Spring Lane,'" and, "oh yes, there are the trees in the garden of my home. Oh! I've got back at last."

I think it will be very like that when we draw really near to our Heavenly Home. We shall remember and recognize the lovely things we left behind when we set out on this strange, wonderful experience of coming to school on earth. It will all seem beautifully familiar.

A little while ago a friend was telling some of us about her grandfather's death. For some reason, almost till the end of his illness, he was filled with fear and dread. At last he even struggled up in the bed, crying out and begging those who were present, to keep him from dying. Then suddenly, he looked up — his face changed, and he exclaimed, "Oh, if it's like that, I want to go!" Then he lay back peacefully in the bed and went.

Yes, when the veil of our physical senses rends apart and the real world begins to appear before us, how glorious it will be!

"When death these mortal eyes shall seal
And still this throbbing heart,
The rending veil shall Thee reveal,
All glorious as Thou art."

It reminds me of a game which we played at a Christmas party when I was a very little girl. I was brought into the drawing room and shown a row of articles of furniture placed down the middle of the room, with the guests arranged on chairs at the sides. The first article was a small table, the next a big chair, the third a bucket of water, and the fourth an umbrella stand. I was told that I was to be blindfolded and then I was to step over all these obstacles, one after the other, without touching a single one. Being a highly nervous child, I protested wildly that it was impossible, and I certainly would not be blindfolded. But two friendly, hefty youths who were present, assured me that they were going to help me. They would stand on each side of me and when I reached each obstacle, they would put their hands under my armpits and lift me and all I had to do was to raise my legs as high as possible, and the impossible feat could then be accomplished. At last I agreed. The blindfold was put over my eyes and I was led forward. "Here is the table, lift your legs right up," cried my two helpers, and they swung me up in the air while I pressed my knees up to my chin. "Well done!" cried all the voices from the sides of the room. "That was simply splendid. Now here is the chair." The process was repeated, up I swung and down I came, and the same thing happened at the pail of water and even when we got to that preposterously tall umbrella stand. There was a great burst of applause, the blindfold was removed from my eyes, and I looked back incredulously down the room and there was not a single dreaded obstacle there. Before I reached each one, someone had silently removed it out of the way! How I did enjoy sitting at the side of the room, watching the next child come in and go through the same hilarious performance! Perhaps the angels love playing that game too! I rather suspect it!

Sometime a wonderful thing is going to happen to me. Something like that described in "The Song of Songs." I shall find myself saying, "I sleep, but my heart waketh; it is the voice of my Beloved that knocketh, saying, Open to Me." No, it will not be Death knocking at the door of my heart, for there is no Death; it has been swallowed up in victory. It will be The Eternal Life Himself, my Lord, my heart's beloved. Into His arms I shall fling myself and go with Him, "further on and higher up" into our Father's World. Let us encourage one another with this glorious hope, and follow the example of that dear Lord Who, "knowing that His hour was come that He should depart out of this world and go to the Father, having loved His own that were in the world, HE LOVED THEM UNTO THE END." John 13:1. Yes; let us concentrate on this glorious ministry of forgetting Self and loving others, and then, when the River is actually reached, we too shall find that we are taken through it "dry shod." For has not our dear Lord said "He that believeth on Me shall never die...He shall never see death." John 11:26, John 8:51.

CPSIA information can be obtained
at www.ICGtesting.com
Printed in the USA
LVHW081244220122
709108LV00013B/1049